"THERE'S A MIRACLE IN YOUR MOUTH"

Life or Death. You Choose

By: Simuel Nathan Hudson Jr.

"There's a Miracle in your Mouth"

Authored by: Simuel Nathan Hudson Jr.

DEDICATION

I dedicate this book to my parents, the late Elder Nathan and Nadine Hudson. A special thanks goes to my Wife Vanessa Hudson. I also want to dedicate this book to my two sons, Simuel Labrian Hudson and Michael Nathan Hudson. A special dedication goes to my late best friend, miss Kimberly Holt's James (Kim).

TABLE OF CONTENTS

INTRODUCTION

Words, Words, Words, yes, everyone uses them every day and all day! From the time we wake up and lay down again, our words fill the atmosphere, provoking attitudes, giving answers, creating proposals, petitions, documents, laws, and contracts. Verbally or written, our words are making vital lifechanging decisions.

It's almost like those long ''app contracts'' online or purchase agreements that we hardly ever read. Yet all of these contracts are binding and legal, so do our words operate in the spiritual realm.

Our Words (in the spiritual realm) are signing life or death contracts. These contracts create healing, blessings, curses, defeat, victory, long life or short life. Words in the spiritual realm operate like contracts and agreements. Words, thoughts, and faith are the original technology of God. Words, in the beginning, were used more for creation than just communication in the origin of humanity.

CHAPTER 1

WORDS ARE EVERYWHERE

Words are the cornerstone of our society, the government, and even our world! Think about it. One way or another, everything is created and operated by WORDS from the heaven's courthouse to your house! Everywhere we look, there are words, words, and more words! Our constitution is WORDS. Our laws are WORDS. Our legal transactions are WORDS. Our marriage, relationships, contracts, agreements, buying cars, property, and giving doctors consent all require our words.

WORDS in thought, WORDS vocalized, or words written control and play a significant role in every part of our lives. Why? Words are ‘’connected’’ to our faith and belief systems accompanied by our imagination. This system was created and first demonstrated by God in Genesis Chapter One. We are shaped by words. Read Genesis 1:26-28. God says He made us in HIS IMAGE AND LIKENESS. Wow! Selah. Stop and think about that for a few days!

CHAPTER 2

OPERATING LIKE GOD

Understand that likeness means we must operate LIKE HIM (GOD)! (Read Genesis Chapter one in the Bible, the creation account). Words heard, spoken, and obeyed invites the spiritual into our natural and physical existence. The spiritual is a place where things that seem or look impossible in the natural realm can become POSSIBLE by accessing the more real and powerful sphere of the spiritual!

The master key in the universe is FAITH expressed by belief, thought, words, and actions. The universe is not in control; the universe obeys us. Actually, everything God made will obey mankind! God created this order when He said in Genesis 1:26-28, "LET THEM (MANKIND) HAVE DOMINION, AUTHORITY, SOVEREIGNTY, CONTROL, and JURISDICTION on the earth." (Psalms 115:16; Psalms 8; Luke 10:17-19).

CHAPTER 3

ORDER AND RANK

God created this order and rank: God first, man and then angels. Often religion and doctrines of devils always attempt to make mankind see ourselves MUCH LOWER than how God sees and created us. Everything God is you are! Everything God can do, you can do!

God is King of kings, but Revelations 1:6 says Jesus Christ has made US kings and priests unto God. John 8:12 says Jesus is the light of the world, but Matthew 5:14-16 says WE are also the light of the world. The Scriptures show Jesus as God, the Word manifested in the flesh, and as God's Son (John 1:1-14). The Scriptures also say WE are gods (PSALMS 82:6), and Jesus said the same thing in John 10:34.

Notice we being gods doesn't mean WE ARE GOD ALMIGHTY OR ELOHIM. But we are His sons. So WE ARE IN THE GOD CLASS, CO-INHERITORS WITH JESUS CHRIST (John 3: 1-3, John 1:12-14, Romans 8:17). We are God's off spring (Acts 17:29) having His attributes and abilities.

Read Psalms 8 (Amp and original Hebrew writings, also Hebrews 2:5-8). The original Hebrew/Greek writings say we were made a little lower than God, NOT angels! Angels have different roles and responsibilities. They are entirely spiritual beings, not in the condemned sinful body as we are at present.

Just because they have remarkable power doesn't mean they outrank us. Authority and rank trumps power! We are seated at the right hand of God with and in Christ Jesus (Ephesians 2:4-6) (Colossians 3:1)! All of these promises and powerful potentials are ONLY EXPERIENCED BY

GRACE & FAITH. They are genuine and real because God, through His word in the Bible, says so. But they will lie dormant in your born again spirit until realized and activated by FAITH. FAITH is NOW (Hebrews 11:1). FAITH is a Master Key.

FAITH is a spiritual principle and law created and given by God to transact operations and creations between heaven and earth or the spiritual and physical arenas.

Faith is from the Greek word pistis, which means to be confident, persuaded, assured, certain of God's Word & HIS power to bring to pass what He has promised. This FAITH Confidence is expressed in primarily three ways.

1. What we say
2. What we pray
3. What or Who we obey (actions)

Faith is the hand that reaches into the supernatural, invisible dimension and lays hold on the promises & power of God! - (1 Peter 1:5)

Be wise & sober always because faith is a spiritual law (Romans 3:27). It can work for you or against you since your belief, actions & words greatly activate it.

Remember Proverbs 18:21 says, “Death and Life are in the power of our tongue.” Our faith will grab either one that we release our Words for!

CHAPTER 4

FAITH

FAITH is the currency of the Kingdom Of God and the Kingdom of darkness. FAITH is a universal, eternal spiritual law (Romans 3:27) that can work for or against you based on your pledged and allegiance to Christ. Also, by the words and actions, you use whether good or bad, no matter what religion you subscribe to.

FAITH is a ''confidence assurance'' and certainty of God's Word, promise, and His ability to bring it to pass; ''Produced'' from hearing, believing, and speaking. THIS FAITH COMES by hearing and hearing, saying and saying, obeying, and obeying as Abraham did in the Bible.

God's Words are alive and living (Hebrews 4:12). God is His Word (John 1:1-2). God and His Word are INSEPARABLE! If you can get it and believe with Faith, God's word and promises are the same as having God Himself in person there with you.

YOU HAVE GOD and His power available through Faith! 1 Peter 1:5 says we are kept by GOD'S power THROUGH FAITH. Ephesians 2:8 says we are saved by Grace but THROUGH FAITH. Read Hebrews Chapter 11, known as the HALL OF FAITH. See the miracles that were accomplished by FAITH!

Sarah was barren but received power to conceive a child when she was far past the childbearing age BY FAITH. Lion's mouths were closed BY FAITH. Dead children were brought back BY FAITH. Men were thrown into the fire but not burned BY FAITH.

We understand BY FAITH, Enoch was caught up without seeing death BY FAITH. Noah built the Ark by saving his family and himself BY FAITH. Faith is the connector! The conduit! The channel! The key! God's power is invited and allowed through Faith in His Word's of promise! His power and life are in His Word, Logos, and Rhema Word!

Especially the Rhema, it's the Rhema Word, which is a word spoken out of the Spirit or received from the Spirit of God. The Rhema is a right now, real-time, commanded spoken word of God from God to our Spirit or through the prophetic utterances of others. Rhema is the Word heard in Romans 10:17, which says Faith comes by hearing and hearing by the WORD RHEMA, not logos but RHEMA of God!

Preachers should be preaching just as much Rhema as the logos, which is the written Word. Sadly most have only the letter of the law, dead Scriptures without the Spirit and breath of God, which promotes bondage and death.

You can tell when you hear just the letter of the law. It hobbles your hopes, diminishes your dreams, poisons, paralyzes your pursuits, and leaves you stuck just waiting for defeat and death. This Rhema, a right now commanded spoken Word from God, is why Abraham finally left his father's house and family and followed Jehovah God's instructions.

Read Genesis 12:1-4. Abram believed God, and got blessed. He was made wealthy by God, so Abraham became a generational and perpetual portal for THE BLESSING to all!

It was a Rhema word that Jesus spoke to Peter in Luke 5:4-7 that gave him the miracle of overflow and abundance in his fishing business that day! God will speak to your Spirit through HIS WORD. Also, through His sent anointed preachers, Apostles, Prophets, and Angels!

John 1:1, 2 says in the beginning, THE WORD WAS the WORD. THE WORD WAS WITH GOD, AND THE WORD WAS GOD! God's life and Spirit reside in HIS WORD and God's Word is quick, powerful, operative, life-giving, and sharper than a double-edged sword!

John 6:63, Hebrew 4:12 reminds us that GOD'S WORD is in our hearts, mouths, prayers, praise, conversations, etc. IT IS A SWORD AND SHIELD IN THE SPIRITUAL REALM (Ephesians 6: 15-18).

That's why the Word says let EVERYTHING WE DO BE DONE in and with Jesus' approval and in His name! What we pray, speak, and obey operates as the receiving and releasing of God's will & Authority IN THE EARTH!

JOB 22:28 says YOU shall decree a thing AND IT SHALL BE ESTABLISHED AND LIGHT, ILLUMINATION, ANSWERS TO QUESTIONS will shine upon YOU and your way!

For example: Begin to DECREE: I shall live and not die. I AM STRONG IN THE LORD. I AM BLESSED. I HAVE GOOD SUCCESS. I HAVE A LONG

STRONG HEALTHY, WEALTHY, ABUNDANT, AND RICH ANOINTED GOD PLEASING LIFE! Daily change your words.

As you begin this revolution by changing your words, you will begin to see your perspectives, situations, and conditions be greatly influenced and changed! This must become a lifestyle, not just a one time act. Watch the revelation, ideas, and knowledge about living, healing, health, wealth, victory, and good success come to you from God's SPIRIT to the inside of your Spirit.

CHAPTER 5

SPEAK THE WORD

The Word received "IN US" consistently mixed with Faith (believing, saying and obeying) sooner than later will give birth to answers, truth, revelation, miracles, power revealed, and God's knowledge of what He wants and what we need. The words and actions of our Faith are necessary to create and RECEIVE God and our desired results!

Proverbs 18:21 says Death and Life are produced, allowed, given power, and ACCESS, activated by the power of YOUR TONGUE, OUR WORDS GIVE CONSENT IN THE SPIRIT REALM for

God, good, blessing, life, or evil, wicked, defeat, disease, disorder, and CURSES or death.

Luke 10:17-19 reminds us that the realm of the spirit will obey you; Spirits are subject to you in Jesus' name when we come to Jesus as Savior and submit to Him as Lord. Therefore, every human should guard their words because words are spiritual transmitters between the spiritual and natural world, and we as humans are spiritual beings.

WE ARE A SPIRIT THAT LIVES IN A BODY AND POSSESSES A SOUL (1Thessalonians 5:23)!

The Spirit of Faith is operated when we begin to vocalize what we believe, GOOD OR BAD, RIGHT OR WRONG. These perceptions and beliefs begin to shape our reality and bring about manifestation.

In Mark 11:23, Jesus said WHOEVER believes anything in their heart and refuses to doubt and keeps saying what they believe THEY WILL HAVE IT! This truth is incredible but at the same time, dangerous. This Spiritual law is at work for everyone all the time no matter your religion, color, or culture. Whether your belief or communication is good or bad, death or life, influenced by heaven or hell this law is working.

There is more power and DOMINION for good, life, and BLESSINGS when we are Christian believers speaking ''God's Word'' but this law is working for everyone on earth. Our words are working for us or against us!

Proverbs 6:2 says we are snared and taken captive by the WORDS OF OUR MOUTH!

Proverbs 18:20 says a man's stomach shall be satisfied with the fruit of his mouth and with the increase of HIS LIPS!

CHAPTER 6

MY TESTIMONY

The Good News translation Bible says, "YOU WILL HAVE TO LIVE WITH THE CONSEQUENCES OF EVERYTHING YOU SAY!" Psalms 34:12-13 (AMPC) says, "What man is he who desires life and longs for many days, that he may see and experience good in those days? 13. KEEP YOUR TONGUE, your words, your conversations from evil and YOUR lips from speaking deceit!" Don't give an evil report. Don't agree with sin or negative news. ONLY SAY THE RESULTS YOU WANT. ONLY SAY GOD'S WORD PROMISE AND REPORT!

Here's a testimony of mine from years ago when visiting the dentist. They did initial cleaning and exams of my teeth and gums. Growing up, we never went to the dentist. So, according to the dentist, my teeth and gums were in bad shape. They looked good and clean on the surface but beneath needed repair. The dentist began treating me 2 to 4 times a year and eventually suggested surgery. He said my teeth and gums WOULD never get better but would continuously become worse and worse.

I'm not against doctors or medications, but I believed God and that nature provides better remedies. I'm not all that excited about any part of my body being opened up and cut on. That's just me. So I remembered a book I had read by Charles Capps about the power of the tongue and some things God had been teaching me over the years. So I began each morning when I got up, I'd go to the bathroom mirror and begin to speak. I did not pray but spoke to my mouth, teeth, gum, and roots! I would tell them what the dentist said about them. Then I would tell my teeth,

"But I believe the Word of God that by Jesus stripes teeth, gums, roots, you are ''healed'' (Isaiah 53:4,5). You are not getting worse, but going from strength to strength, becoming better and better (Psalms 84:12,13)!

I would use a few other words of healing, but I was commanding my teeth, gums, and roots to line up with God's truth, not man's or the dentist's facts! So I continued my visits to the dentist, and over a few months, I would always ask the dentist how are they looking, and he would say, "Simuel, they are not going to get better without the surgery."

I continued my morning rituals of SPEAKING TO MY MOUNTAINS (Mark 11:23): My teeth, gums, and roots. Now, after months went by at the dentist's office, they took X-rays of my mouth. I noticed the nurse looking at the x-rays strangely. Then she called another nurse or technician in. They stood there looking at my x-rays.

Finally, they both went and got the dentist, and he stood there with them looking at the sets of x-rays; I'll never forget that day. Then, he looked at me and asked, "Mr. Hudson, what have you been doing differently to your teeth?" I said, "Nothing really. I floss and brush as you told me every day, and I have been praying for my teeth and gums."

I was too embarrassed to say I talked to my teeth, roots, and gums, but I thought he might understand praying for them better. He looked at the x-rays again and looked at me and said, "Whatever you're doing, keep doing." Then he showed me the x-rays from before and that day.

He showed me on the x-rays how my roots had begun to reset or restructured and got better! Remember, this same dentist told me my teeth, roots, and gums would never get better. There's a miracle in your mouth and wonders to perform through the power of your Words!

This is why Proverbs 4:23 says to guard our hearts above ALL ELSE because the issues of life come from and through YOUR HEART AND SPIRIT initiated by Words, information, exposures, and influences. These become our truth once we believe them. it doesn't matter if they're right or wrong from God or Satan. YOU AND YOUR WORDS ARE THE catalysts!

I have learned life isn't happening to us but THROUGH US! Read 2 Corinthians 4:13, Mark 11:23-25, and Genesis Chapter 1. God used His Words, His Faith, His Imagination, and His Thoughts, which released into the SPIRIT and began to create what God thought, said, and commanded TO BE!

Read Hebrews 1: 3 - John 1:1-14. God's Word should always be the final authority and deciding factor for what we base decisions on, believe, pray, say, and obey! God's will for our personal lives DOES NOT come to pass automatically, but only by us being intentional, on purpose, and belief, PRAYING, SAYING, OBEYING, confession, and obedience to the Word and Spirit of the living God.

Results may not always manifest overnight, but with patient persistence in our ''Faith Fight'' and an ever listening ear to the Spirit of God and an obeying heart, VICTORY IS INEVITABLE! Be blessed, ARMOR ON, PURSUE AND POSSESS, OCCUPY TILL CHRIST RETURNS! Your body, mind, family, community, business, and ministry is a part of your TERRITORY, COVER IT AND THEM WITH THE SAVING SHIELD OF FAITH! There's a miracle in your mouth!

ABOUT THE AUTHOR

Simuel Nathan Hudson Jr. was Born March 3rd, 1971, to Elder Nathan & Nadine Hudson. A father to two sons: Simuel Labrian Hudson and Michael Nathan Hudson. Simuel has been involved in ministry and music in some capacity all of his life. Whether playing and singing for his father's radio broadcast as a child or pastoring, preaching or doing conferences. Also, doing radio and some TV ministry.

Serving has been a big part of Simuel's life. Simuel is also a recording artist, songwriter, and producer with three recorded music projects to date and prophetic singles all available on Amazon and YouTube. Currently, Prophet Simuel Nathan Jr. is the founder of The School of the Prophets, a ministry for equipping future Kingdom Leaders, especially Prophets and Prophetic Ministers and Leaders.

Prophet Simuel was chosen and called by the Lord for such a time as this. He is a prophetic teacher of the gospel and a man of Godly humility. This man of God is a man of worship and worships the Lord with passion and believes in the power of prayer and faith in God!

He desires to see God's people healed and delivered and living a Kingdom victorious life before the Father. Prophet Simuel Nathan Hudson Jr. was licensed as a minister in 1998. Ordained as Pastor in 2009 and set in the office of the Prophet in 2012. Prophet Simuel has been functioning in ministry for about 22 years. He is the father of two boys.

If the writings of this book blessed you, be sure to check out his first and second book, which is now available on Amazon: ''My First Conversation With God'' and Process Before Progress ''Somethings Only Come After.''

Contact Information
Facebook @ Simuel Nathan Jr.
Email: Simuelhudson@gmail.com
Contact number: 770-560-0994

www.ingramcontent.com/pod-product-compliance
Ingram Content Group UK Ltd.
Pitfield, Milton Keynes, MK11 3LW, UK
UKHW021644190726
13853UKWH00001B/35

9 798512 901892